T0058031

The Road In Is Not the Same Road Out

THE ROAD IN IS NOT
THE SAME ROAD OUT

— — — —

KAREN SOLIE

— — — —

FARRAR STRAUS GIROUX

NEW YORK

FARRAR, STRAUS AND GIROUX

120 BROADWAY, NEW YORK 10271

COPYRIGHT © 2015 BY KAREN SOLIE

ALL RIGHTS RESERVED

ORIGINALLY PUBLISHED IN 2015 BY
HOUSE OF ANANSI PRESS, CANADA
PUBLISHED IN THE UNITED STATES IN 2015
BY FARRAR, STRAUS AND GIROUX
FIRST AMERICAN PAPERBACK EDITION, 2016

THE LIBRARY OF CONGRESS HAS CATALOGED THE
HARDCOVER EDITION AS FOLLOWS:
SOLIE, KAREN, 1966–
[POEMS. SELECTIONS]
THE ROAD IN IS NOT THE SAME ROAD OUT : POEMS /
KAREN SOLIE. — FIRST AMERICAN EDITION.
PAGES CM
ISBN 978-0-374-29850-0 (HARDCOVER) —
ISBN 978-0-374-71358-4 (EBOOK)
I. TITLE.
PR9199.4.S695 A6 2015
811'.6—DC23

2014043837

PAPERBACK ISBN: 978-0-374-53616-9

DESIGNED BY QUEMADURA

OUR BOOKS MAY BE PURCHASED IN BULK FOR PROMOTIONAL,
EDUCATIONAL, OR BUSINESS USE. PLEASE CONTACT
YOUR LOCAL BOOKSELLER OR THE MACMILLAN CORPORATE
AND PREMIUM SALES DEPARTMENT AT 1-800-221-7945,
EXTENSION 5442, OR BY EMAIL AT
MACMILLANSPECIALMARKETS@MACMILLAN.COM.

WWW.FSGBOOKS.COM
WWW.TWITTER.COM/FSGBOOKS
WWW.FACEBOOK.COM/FSGBOOKS

FOR MY FRIENDS

CONTENTS

The Road In Is Not the Same Road Out

ODE

Blue jay vocalizes a clash on the colour
wheel, tulip heads removed one by one

with a sand wedge. Something
in the frequency. Expectations are high.

There's a reason it's called the nervous
system. Someone in bed at 11 a.m.

impersonates an empty house. The sharpener's
dragged his cart from the shed. His bell

rings out from the twelfth century
to a neighbourhood traumatizing

food with dull knives. A hammer claws
to the edge of a reno and peers over. Inching

up its pole, a tentative flag. And the source?
Oh spring, my heart is in my mouth.

– – –

THE CORNERS

Where the question are you alright usually finds one very much
not alright. Cellphone at the bus stop, cellophane, wind,
Hasty Mart in its collar of pigeon spikes. With smokes
in front of the sports bar, careerists mid-shift lit at dusk
by the inner light of cheap bottles
of domestic. Like payphones, cords have been cut
that tied them to the world. Let me off in the primary
neighbourhood, I'll walk the traffic's bank,
its decorative plantings and contradictory signage, the current,
I can't brave it. Fortunes approach right-angled in their vehicles
of delivery, hearts beat quickly in anticipation
or dread inspired by the landmarks. How long have I resided
in these years of gentrification and not realized
they're gone—the inconvenient, inadequate, or taken
for granted? The psychic welcomes no more walk-ins
in this life. Time is short. Though a timeless sublegal
entrepreneurial spirit flourishes over which laundromats preside
geologically, with deep sighs, belying
with the state of their drains their adjectives. No one

— — —

can be alone like they can. Pedestrians, obey your signals.
On the boulevard of a two-stage crossing he reads in her
an imminent change in direction. We were here once,
hand in hand at the intersection of the cardinal and ordinal,
blessed with purpose, and the Star of Poland still in business.

— — —

RENTAL CAR

It's not a contract until the names are on it.
Though always there is one who signs off with less
than a whole heart. "Leading Today for Tomorrow,"
that's Mississauga's slogan. Or is it "leaving" . . .
eastbound, westbound, exodus via
the 400-series highways. Personal reasons
I will not get into. The 427 interchange
is a long note in space, flightpath of materials
the grace of which is a reason to live. Is not likewise
the possibility and mortal danger of shooting
its photograph from the roadbed? Is not digital

radio? Accelerate into the curve by the Ford plant,
its freshly birthed Fusions in the nursery lot
behind razorwire, their cradle the duplication
of goods and services. Oakville's motto is "Go Forward."
And, indeed, where is everyone? They are shopping
in the Dixie Mall because their cars are there.
They're working in pharmaceutical company offices

- - -

because their cars are there. They're eating
at the golf club. They're lying in their beds. Burlington
is "The Home of Ribfest." Upon the satellite campus
of the Lancaster Gentlemen's Club,

sodium haloes cast an abiding light
whose influence fades along the paved
and shouldered avenues locals call country roads.
We are all locals now. A thing is what it is called.
Country has become the countryside.
It gets so you don't want to talk about it,
though the air is thick with personal messaging.
A thought could walk on it as on stones to find you.
My good horse will bear me over the river
of that noise. As through a burning cloud
my good horse will carry me.

FABLES OF THE RECONSTRUCTION

Nose down in their day of rest. Bobcat, excavator, trackhoe
on legislated hiatus from the business of holes and
fill, of avoiding gaslines and the inadvertent manufacture
of larger holes, budget overrun, a public relations nightmare.
No rest, though, for he who must negotiate such obstacles,
rolling his cart and its empties toward refund, refill,
toward reinforcing the gaps in his memory. Who will attend
to whether his solitude is taken up in pleasure
or despair? He is a hole in the landscape. He is a black bird
at night. The security cameras of Queen Street have suffered
violent ends, and record the pit of their disconnection.

Images supplied by recollection inspire little confidence.
Lab techs riding herd on experimental krill and bright exotics
like high B-flats in the middle C of the faux environment
were stumped by consecutive disappearances
of these regulated populations. No evidence,
no earthly remainder. Should a single being vanish into
what is not, so all things may vanish, as is written.

— — —

Commence to tremble. Then rig the lab cam. Witness
the octopus crawl out of his tank to feast, retreat before shift
the next day. They took him away. Why wouldn't you
recognize the divine in him? It's difficult to commit injustice
and elude detection, said Epicurus,
but to be confident of eluding detection is impossible.
He also said life is ruined by delay.

The animal dies when the soul withdraws. Dion Phaneuf
has been traded to the Maple Leafs. Neck deep in a Calgary
piano bar, the future of the franchise attempts "Piano Man,"
but can't get past the first verse. Soon, he might as well have
been born there. Sings it again and again, infernal recurrence
without beginning or end, as the Acme Portable Hole
reaffirms its nomination as the best thing never invented.
Crowd studded with cameraphones like a ham with cloves.
Now always we look upon ourselves. Beauty and terror
in equal measure. Intrigue of a boarded-up building.
We want to get in there and find out what's the matter with it.

— — —

A WESTERN

Its origins are to this hour undetermined.
The free-floating found
its transformative agent. A third term
arose. It was a thing, it existed.

Not a friend, though in all other things
it did kindle a renewed existence.
Storefronts said, *defend yourself.*
Under pavements, the timbers,
arms around one another, said
embrace your condition, said, *we are lost.*

Equipment is in a peculiar position.
It knows it belongs to the earth.
The machine, with its thousand parts,
is a thing, as is its smallest bearing.
A pail is a thing. So is
the water it carries. A painting
hangs like a hat on a nail.

- - -

Judgement, perception, death are things
in themselves; they're not nothing,
though they don't, as things, appear.

But what is the use of a feeling, however
certain, in defining that which itself
is only a feeling? No thing
can survive such boredom.
The situation prevails with its timeline.

A third term arose between us, it existed.
But a violence has been done
to its element it could not withstand.
It is not dead, unseen, or elsewhere.
Nothing real any longer corresponds to it.

Above the harbour a gull creates flight
as flight has created him. He arises
and results from his work.
He is the circle that violates logic.
That's where his soul is.

– – –

WHEN ASKED WHY HE'D BEEN TALKING TO HIMSELF, PYRRHO REPLIED HE WAS PRACTICING TO BE A NICE FELLOW

Carrying my ladder to the next jobsite, I may get you one way
turning to identify your voice, and the other
as I resume my path. It isn't personal,
merely aluminum and telescopic. The feet of my ladder
will be planted on the earth, its hands
in the branches of the stars.
History steadies it and will not be persuaded otherwise.
From its topmost I contemplate oilsands, acts of
war, abandoned dogs sobbing in confusion
and grief, the correlative of which is all the world's joy.
A fear follows, if experience holds,
one's inner badger stuck in one's inner drain.
But that's another life disowned, more surely absent now
than what has never come to pass: the great

— — —

accomplishments of my youth, say.

It only looks like I'm not working.

My atoms, like yours, like those of bamboo forests and Bakelite

are in constant motion, which should suffice for one day

to keep us from killing each other or falling in love

with our respective essential mysteries.

We can acknowledge the tulip's beauty without eating

its poisonous bulb, admire the geometry

of the dodecahedron and not waste our lives

in a rec room at role-playing games.

It's said when septic medicines, surgical and caustic procedures

were applied to Pyrrho's wounds, he didn't so much as

frown. Let us not agree carelessly about important matters.

The death of your cockatiel and the shearing

of an Antarctic glacier the size of Manhattan are events

differing only in kind. For those who pledge definitively

and confidently, a curse inevitably ensues. Sometimes

when I've thought I've hurt you,

you haven't even noticed I'm around. I admire that.

It's something one might work toward one's whole life.

AFFIRMATIONS

Has the past not pursued me with its face
and haven't I turned away?
Can a thing made once not be made again?

Hasn't the rider returned to her horse,
the dog to his master? Isn't this the lesson
of our popular literature?
And was the trash not collected
this morning, signalling no disruption
to the civic schedule?

Isn't the gesture, the act, inarguable?
And don't we live a parallel life in thought,
an attentiveness not unlike

a natural prayer of the mind and not-mind?
The shadow cast between them.
Where an unlight burns.

- - -

Won't nighttime reawaken and won't it be familiar?
Unequivocal through Carolinian forests
which have not wholly disappeared,
and equally among rows
of wrecked cars in the junkyards,
hoods open like a choir?

MUSEUM OF THE THING

Sad storm of objects becoming things,
the objective correlative, tired of me
as I am of it. I embody everything it hates
about itself. People don't stand in for each other

the way things do. Someone
for whom Wednesday means groceries
might animate Wednesday with, among other
realities, the inability to possess it,

as one might a derelict potato chip factory
co-opted to ventriloquize one's state
of mind. It's impossible to know, entirely,
what a trip to the Real Canadian Superstore

suggests to someone else. Even animals,
notoriously difficult to work with,
whose very mention in this context invites
derision, illuminate a failure of perception

— — —

no less uninformative for being true.
It does not satisfy. Dear being, how might I
responsibly interpret your incomprehensible
behaviour? Where am I in it?

The imagination, whole yet incomplete,
feels its edges. Gestures from its windows
as if into a city whose language no one speaks.
A dilemma unresolvable, but mutual.

– – –

THE WORLD

When I learned I could own a piece of The World
I got my chequebook out. Eternal life belongs to those
who live in the present. My wife's bright eye affirmed it.
As do the soothing neutral tones and classic-contemporary
decor of our professionally designed apartments,
private verandahs before which the globe, endlessly
and effortlessly circumnavigated, slips by, allowing residents
no end of exotic ports, a new destination every few days
to explore with a depth we hadn't thought possible.
It's not how things are on The World that is mystical,
not the market and deli, proximity of masseuse
and sommelier, not the gym, our favourite restaurant,
our other favourite restaurant, the yacht club, the library,
the golf pro, the pool, but that it exists at all, a limited
whole, a logic and a feeling. What looks like freedom
is, in fact, the perfection of a plan, and property
a stocktaking laid against us in a measure. The difference
between a thing thought, and done. One can ignore neither
the practical applications nor the philosophical significance

— — —

of our onboard jewelry emporium, its $12 million inventory,
natural yellow diamonds from South Africa no one needs,
thus satisfying the criteria for beauty. Without which
there is no life of the mind. What we share, though, transcends
ownership, our self-improvement guaranteed
by the itineraries, licensed experts who prepare us
for each new harbour and beyond, deliver us into the hands
of native companions on The World's perpetual course.
The visual field has no limits. And the eye—
the eye devours. Polar bears, musk oxen, rare thick-billed
murre. We golfed on the tundra and from The World
were airlifted to pristine snowfields, clifftops where we dined
alfresco above frozen seas. The World is the entirety.
The largest ship ever to traverse the Northwest Passage.
How the silent energy coursed between us. Fundamental rules
had changed. Except, with time, it seems a sort of accident—
natural objects combined in states of affairs, their internal
properties. Accusatory randomness and proliferation
of types, brutal quantity literally brought to our doors.
Or past them, as if on the OLED high-def screen
of our circumstances, which hides more than it reveals.
For what we see could be other than it is.
Whatever we're able to describe at all could be other
than it is. Such assaults on our finer feelings require an appeal

- - -

to order, to the exercise of discipline a private Jacuzzi represents,

from which one might peacefully enjoy the singular euphoria

of the Panama Canal or long-awaited departure

from fetid Venice. There is some truth in solipsism, but I fear

I'm doing it wrong, standing at the rail for ceremonial cast-offs

thunderously accessorized with Vangelis or "Non, je ne regrette

rien,"

made irritable by appreciative comments about the light.

In Reykjavík or Cape Town, it's the same. Familiarity

without intimacy is the cost of privacy, security

of a thread count so extravagant its extent can no longer

be detected. Even at capacity, The World is eerily empty:

its crew of highly trained specialists in housekeeping,

maintenance, beauty, and cuisine—the heart and soul

of the endeavour—are largely unseen and likely where the fun is.

We sit at the captain's table but don't know him. He's Italian.

I think on my Clarksville boyhood long before EPS, ROE—

retractable clothesline sunk in concrete, modest backyard

a staging ground for potential we felt infinite to the degree

our parents knew it wasn't. The unknown is where we played.

And while fulfilment of a premeditated outcome

confers a nearly spiritual comfort of indifference

to the time of year, a paradise of fruits always in season,

the span of choice defines its limit, which cannot be exceeded.

— — —

The sea rolls over, props on an elbow, and now is heard
the small sound of a daydream running softly aground.
Dissatisfaction, in a Danish sense. On prevailing winds a scent
of compromise; for one tires of the spacewalk outside
what is the case. Beyond immediate luxuries
lives speculation and the tragic impression one is yet
to be born. It could be when all pursuits have been satisfied,
life's problems will remain untouched. But doubt exists only
where questions exist. The World satisfies its own conditions.
It argues for itself. Herein lies an answer.

Gratitude toward the houseplants, shame
for what they must endure. Of particular concern,
the azalea, flowering like the gestures and cries
of someone off the trail who sees a helicopter.
A long cold night is coming on.

Is it dying or being killed?
When I'm 100 percent on what's happening,
there's still that niggling five. Too much
water, neglect, information. Decisions
made at the executive level.

Science tells us plants emit signatures and responses
on yet another frequency we cannot hear.
That's all we need. When little,
we were told our heads were in the clouds.
Now we suspect the opposite.

– – –

CHILDHOOD TRIPTYCH

I

Whether I'd seen them with, so to speak, my own eyes
was not the point. I may have filed some false reports,
but I'd seen plenty. Many nights they summoned me
in their fraudulent Rapture, discriminating not between
creatures and objects lifted equally into unbelonging
and returned with forms, that is, spirits,
broken. Before the world destroys us, it confirms
our suspicions. And so I kept my incredulity at the irreparable
local disdain for storm cellars to myself, investing instead
in superstition and my firstborn birthright
of being consistently wrong. As atmospheric hydraulics
once more engaged and the home acre prepared to revolve
like a sickening restaurant, as the grain's hairs stood
on end and rope ladders descended from the gospels'
green windows, my mother, in the manner of someone
who believes wholeheartedly in God's love and its profound
uselessness, said we'd take our chances in the basement.

- - -

II

It was always morning. Premonition like iodine in water
or the smell of malathion and there they were, corrupting
our rural airspace with 1970s speculative anachronism
and the analogue synth that represented the future.
They hovered appreciatively over operational secrets
of junkpile and chickenhouse as our quorum unfolded
its debate at a clear disadvantage intelligence-wise.
If little else, we affirmed the hubris of the Slavic character,
and hoped the Russians were happy now, having broadcast
into the godforsaken interplanetary void a Morse message
like a wren flushed from the bush we were hiding under.
They weren't fitting in. Simply curious, we hoped,
even friendly, though we weren't particularly either.
We almost got used to them. Until the altered pitch
and pneumatic exposure of a new bit of gear we'd known
in our hearts was there, and the shooting started.
My dream people, real to themselves, ran screaming.

– – –

Presumably profiting from the same virus raising the dead
in theatres then, they were days crossing the prairie,
the old joke turned inside out, an antique pace
through pasture and crop assigned by disfigurements
and dislocations of their martyrdom: burned, flayed, minus
hands and feet, exposed to wild beasts, flung headlong from
high places, transfixed, and not in a good way. Catherine
of Alexandria—as featured in the collectible card series
Sister Rose distributed in class to illustrate parables
proving the less-than-evident value of thinking
for the long term—held her disagreeable head before her.
When your heart has been broken, nothing can stop you.
A touchy lot, they didn't look purified. We made an inventory
of our weapons, which is our way of keeping calm.
There seemed ample time to do what we needed to, given
virtues of the age. But here are the saints already among us,
anxious to communicate the burden of being chosen.

- - -

BE REASONABLE

My husband says to set the legs of our bed
in buckets of water is to overreact.
He does not subscribe to the online bedbug registry.
Does not acknowledge on his tactical map the advance
from the Delta, the Odeon, incubation in the warm folds of the
   greater
film industry, in homeless shelter and the public
upholsteries. A sideboard proclaiming itself free at the curbside
is a Trojan horse. On our street,
posts from #83, then #96, where it's reported the landlady presents
with an aggressive strain of denial and poor interpersonal skills.
Not my business? They make it my business.

Often I don't recognize what I'd rather not do until I've agreed to
   do it.
Then I know what I want and what I want makes me weak.
I grew up comforted by coyotes in the evening, but the news
from the suburbs is be afraid.
It seems you can live your whole life with a creature

- - -

and only know it one way. The pine beetle and rusty grain beetle
don't realize the harm they do, they are only having experiences.
I didn't want to kill the house spiders but they died
in my engagement with the larger project.
The spray bottle of dimethyl benzyl ammonium chloride is
    empty.
Once I leave the room, the job will be finished.

- - -

From the airplane, fields are an Eric Cameron—
Reds and Yellows on Green—a process
begun as innovation now manifest
in the monoculture. Silent Lake
from an airplane is apprehended
geographically, with visible parameters,
but is all surface, like the past. The future
is an airplane seen from an airplane.

Lorazepam's sweet fog has burned off.
Here is the present, its landing gear.
And the absence of someone
whose participation as such
is largely involuntary.

March, and the capital lights one dim lamp.
Its restaurants are closed; its thoughts, inward.
The fat of its heart has been spent on winter.

— — —

In the National Gallery all the seeds of colour
are preserved. Lit like a mountain
laboratory, its concrete architectural prologue
aspires to stone in the floodlights.
Chambers, anterooms, great halls, rotunda, dome,
restaurant, theatre, gift shop, inside is a landscape
of the unconscious mind.

I can't find the elevator with the map
I've been given. Around the corner of every era,
every great advancement in perspective, the same
security guard and the twentieth century
is being rehung.

Joshua Reynolds, show me the way,
you whose career, all due respect, never
peaked, but who painted until your eyes
gave out. Your Colonel Charles Churchill,
visual allegories to hand, stares wanly
and imperfectly past the elements
of composition, like a ghost after the fugitive
carmine of his living complexion, another victim
of the experiment. Though the experiment
continues as he fades and is a kind of life.
Our eyes meet in the frame.

- - -

Back at the hotel, a message waits,
received through the crowded air's invisible
wires. The message is a liquid crystal display.
Distance's droning lecture on policy is interrupted.
Doors of the long grey hall fly open.

ROTHKO VIA MUNCIE, INDIANA

The 1980s. Beginning of the long decade, the century's
late works. Snow on the grid, field bisected
by a new-model John Deere's progress in low gear
with a front-end load of straw bales. Its operator's daughter
dons her brace, thinks her scoliosis the devil's work
on her, a not-good-enough Christian. Her mother talks
scripture on the phone in the kitchen and the kitchen
smells of coffee and it smells of dog. Christmas lights

strung along the eaves of bungalows, vehicles moored
to bungalows by their block heater cords. Rumours
of drunkenness and corruption sunk the Democrat's bid
for mayor. *For we favour the simple expression of the complex*
thought. The large shape's impact of the unequivocal. Flat forms
that destroy illusion and reveal truth. Now the union's eye
has twilight in it, and the city dump will stay where it is.
Evening falls, or rises, or emanates from the figures.
The SportsPlex and Model Aviation Museum, the Muncie
Mall and both quadrangles of Ball State University

- - -

shed their associations, perform an unknown adventure
in unknown space. Halogens illuminate an anecdote
of the spirit. You won't see his face around here again.
The violet quarry hosts a greater darkness further in,
the White River sleeps in its cabin of pack ice.
Among the graduating class an abstract feeling develops,

an inclination to symbolism born of the fatal car wreck on
New Year's, a spike in requests for Bob Seger
to the call-ins from a quasi-religious experience of limitless
immensity. To achieve this clarity is inevitably
to be misunderstood. Their lives take on the dimensions
of the fields, the city, its facades and its plan, whose happiness
will be their own. Rent, food budget, sweaters
indoors. Basketball, basketball, and a second marriage.

INTERIOR

after Jack Chambers

Neither question nor assertion makes sense
when truth is a tone of voice. As if I were a wall,
    a former life
           walks through me, each
      modest architectural feature
           an anthology of meanings to which paint
has been applied. They don't retain
traces, that's in thinking.

One would do well to adopt
a chemically pure standpoint
    of appraisal, to lay down the repairs
           and cleaning cloths, to set aside the plan —
    there is no plan.
As object of exchange and economic indicator,
    it entertains no hopes for us, is escorted
by its infestations back to ground.

Wind plays through its failings. Basement
cells divide toward the water table. The roof
      maintains no argument
      with rain, with shortcuts in
           construction, the storm's many elements
as the one true storm.
      Evergreens, off-street parking, clouds at dusk
      like clouds in western art.

The gardener, after a time,
feels the garden belongs to him,
      familiar objects extend
his spirit: *a malady expressed by drowsiness.*
      Wind moves likewise the feather and the ash.
      You are the spirits, you are the dust.
        Take them with you into the astonishing
      night alien to us both.

MOLE

Those new flagstones need undermining,
the concrete sundial could use a tilt and while he's at it
he'll make a disaster of the borders. His order
is not our order. He prays to his own ingenuity. His desires
feature a plump worm larder and gathering
the tender beechnuts while ducking horrors the surface
churns out: cat-things, dog-things, pellet guns, poison,
trowels to flip him over the fence into the neighbour's
as though that doesn't hurt. It doesn't work for us,
his gross body plan, eyes skinned shut and his front feet
hands, polydactylic and psychoanalytically proportioned
in that they are oversized and hairless. He does not require
an afterlife. When the consequence whose birth
we've outsourced, reared *extra-muros* on the output
of our comfort zone, comes of age, he'll rejoin
his live/work situation as manager and sole proprietor
of our old estates. He'll raise each molehill like a flag.
In the morning the lawn will be a field of victory.

— — —

VIA

Only through the train window is the idle backhoe
figurative, do electrical transformers astride
the fine and dwindling farmland pause
spellbound in their march toward the lakeshore.

At Oakville's irritable limits, hills of scrap aluminum glitter
like a picnic ground in heaven. No one gets on or off
at Ingersoll. Aldershot, Woodstock, Glencoe, Chatham
came of age in the corridor. It remembers where cars

and appliances came from when they came
from there, witnesses the fate of plastics
and obsolete electronics purchased
at big-box developments pinning the new grids down.

Whose architectures are illiterate, but whose lots
are full. Some good jobs have returned,
though diminished, untrustworthy in their refusal to commit,
and withholding benefits. They must be lived with

– – –

or left. Descendants of these unions construct
rumours, tributes, territorial admonishments
in fatcap and wildstyle on overpass and soundfence,
life-sized, largely unreadable at speed, though a sense

of form lingers. Of colour. Old service roads
partnered with criminal opportunism end
in abandoned lots, tears, and assurances
to the contrary. I never meant to hurt anyone.

No parties in formal wear await us at the stations,
no family vacations. Here are creosote and allergies,
energy drinks, your fellow passengers:
young mothers, elderly couples, gamers talking shop,

business travellers stuck in the minors, students
clothed in battlefields of competing logos, totally in love
from the neck down. You are a type, too.
Bereft, content, bored witless, anticipatory, according

to your natures, to the capabilities of your remote
devices, deflecting ministrations of a seatmate
with a theory. Or asleep in the mind's room decorated
in the cathode ray's flickering blue, maturing perfume

- - -

of boiled potatoes and 1970s optimism. By now
you're far from home. You've found out
who your friends are. A passing freight
throws a bag over your head, pushes your thoughts over,

roars and clatters at a forearm's distance like the exposed
mechanics of a parallel universe and for a moment
you belong to the ages, without affiliation.
Until the snack trolley arrives to restore you to yourself,

to managers and clerks smoking in solidarity
on loading docks of light industrial areas, to mid-morning
in October, pools of remaindered night on leesides
seeding winter in the vacancies. As you coast

into the original neighbourhoods, ruins imply not
failure, but a lesson in patience. Memorial
to all that will neither be remade nor fall apart
completely. In trackside yards roam brightly

coloured polymers of contemporary
playtime, rainsoaked furnitures of early marriage
left with the question of material integrity.
Playing fields, the Park & Ride, nursing homes

— — —

like ghost ships. Wholesale Monuments. Everywhere,
motives on display, arguments with the ideal,
though it makes no sense to say we've always
played this wrong. One doubt hides another.

A record of our conduct. Standing water. Off-world
junkspace with mysterious distributive protocols,
peevish piles of refuse under a "No Dumping" sign.
For a bit of certainty, you would do anything.

It's no use to look within. These towns,
like your own, lived in or yet to be, are forever inadequate
to the secret self who forges ahead, calls
from beyond any given incorporation, from the fog

into which the railbed steals, with your own,
better voice. It will catch you living somewhere
nearly by accident, but fluently, to all appearances
the station you were born to.

— — —

I LET LOVE IN

When they were together she thought it God's punishment.
When he left she thought it God's punishment.

When vermin overrun the city's boardinghouses
and highrises it's God sticking a hose
into the Devil's hole to flood him out.

And when the floodwaters rose,
where was everyone?

When fog risen from the lake assimilates varietals
of exhaust, evolves through the financial district, renders toxic
the neighbourhoods, swells over suburbs, the Devil
has forsaken another project, saying sometimes
I can't fucking concentrate on anything.

He says he does what he does sometimes because
the Devil gets in like water through his weak places.

— — —

When it rains like now the Devil yells at God
I've told you not to call me that. When it rains like now.
And every time God laughs at this

roofs lift off along the Eastern Seaboard. The Eastern Seaboard
will never understand.

When we are broken, to whom are we opened?

God's taken all the fish home to live with him, honey.

And when the earth shakes that's God rearranging furniture
not a bomb in the subway like we thought.

If you feel the Devil with you, he is there.
If you think God has abandoned you,
you are abandoned, his attention

on the World Series, more important than any one man,
smiting the hell out of the Rangers' big bats as the Giants
lift fingers to the sky in praise and the ordnance
deployed in his name, in making straight the way,
would fill the oceans.

- - -

And each foreclosure is a failure of belief,
each immortal jellyfish a failure of belief.

When those who will ruin us are elected,
where is everyone?

And when I return from the desert it's with the Devil
cast out. With God cast out. Because it wasn't really me

who did those things before, that wasn't me.

— — —

LIFT UP YOUR EYES

It's dark by five. The time of year
we cleave to lightboxes, their travel
versions, and dawn simulators ordered online
from the SADLight Super-Store. West, there is some
daylight left, and later, by the north's lantern, its plains
read in black, white, grey, and lighter
grey, a beauty acknowledged in the animal way
with the whole mind, in a strategy. Distance
lies heavily on that municipality, its roads,
as will the snow, more so now the school has
gone, and the store, closure of which inaugurated
the season and its proprietors' bankruptcy. Neighbours
rallied to keep their electricity on, but when even this
could no longer be done, they moved in
with family in some other town. He'd been back to gather
a few last things—people had seen him there—
and in his daughter's home died of heart attack
that afternoon. I met him once or twice,
it being years since I've lived in that place,

- - -

which like all others is unlike any in the details
of its luck and failures. We hate the one to whom we belong,
and love the one to whom we don't. Winter will say
its long mass over him, over troubled ground upon which
are written the liturgies, the ends of the earth. Anything
going has far to go. As they wandered. I heard the news
on the phone. They'd come from the east coast.

ALL THAT IS CERTAIN IS NIGHT

LASTS LONGER THAN THE DAY

Look at your past, how it's grown.
You've known it since it was yea high. Still you,
as you stand now, have never been there. Parts worn out,
renewed, replaced. Though you may bear the same name.
You're like the joke about the axe.

In time you've learned to behave badly isn't
necessarily to behave out of character. *To thine own self
be true.* In script above the nation's chalkboards,
the nation's talkshows. And not a great idea,
depending. It's too much for you, I know.

One day your life will be a lake in the high country no one
will ever see, and also the animals there, figures
indistinguishable from ground.
All of time will flow into it.

— — —

Leave the child you were alone. The wish to comfort her
is a desire to be comforted. Would you have
her recognize herself buried alive
in the memories of a stranger? Forgo the backroads,
double-wides of friends, and friends of friends . . .
Some of what you would warn against
has not yet entered her vernacular.

She travels unerringly toward you, as if you are the north.
Between you, a valley has opened.
In this valley a river,
on this river an obscuring mist.

A mist not unlike it walks the morning streets, comments on
the distinction of Ottawa from Hull, Buda
from Pest, what used to be Estuary from what used to be
Empress, the ferry that once ran between them.

KEEBLEVILLE

Sausage makers, salt farmers, whose wives and daughters
smoked menthols. Their bake sales baffling displays
of unexplainable choices. They'd built themselves
an indoor pool by 1979. We had none. Our curriculum
embraced partnership for the sake of our physical
education, so each swimming lesson was a lesson in defeat.
Our cries rang off the Quonset hut's corrugated steel.

As our school failed, theirs thrived, its sprung wood gym floor,
ceiling domed and beamed, classrooms around a mezzanine,
they wielded it like an unassailable proof, assaulted us
with it. All in that ridiculous accent, the inexplicable
outfits. Now our school is gone. Where once we fought them
in the parking lots, the arenas, left our blood and teeth
in the arenas, on the street in front of the bar, after band concerts
and ball tournaments and grad, and sometimes during,
now must we compel our children to be bused there,
to disembark the Blue Bird like prisoners on work detail.

- - -

Will our heirs go on to name their own after the wrong
soap opera characters and country music stars? Thirteen miles
down the road, and you'd think it another planet, a hostile
one, or overly friendly, in any case backward and impossible
to understand. No doubt, they'd say the same about us.
Which only serves to confirm what I've been telling you.

BIRTH OF THE RIFLE

Gunpowder in the water or wine, the willow
charcoal, potassium nitrite crystals emergent
in manure, barrel in the ground and stock in the tree,

and a new mechanism flowers along the Danube,
along the Rhine. Power without accuracy
is a triumph of unreason. He shot

the passenger window out. Thought it was down
and saw a skunk through it. An idea of the good life
for a person must be based on the nature

of that person. From the Pennsylvania colony
through the Cumberland Gap, by the Rockcastle
River and the Dix, Daniel Boone carried

what was named in his honour. It leans on the seat
of the half-ton where the girlfriend sits
on weekends. It leans in a corner by the screen door,

— — —

avoiding the federal registry. Pursuant to the protection
of individual rights against the common purpose
of our enemies. Your dinner does not willingly relinquish

its spirit, whose shape remains, whose qualities
are eliminated. Survival relies on the subordination
of non-rational aspects. River Forth, Water

of Leith from whence Patrick Ferguson brought
his breech-loading flintlock and was shot through the elbow
during the American Revolution. Eternal rest

by the Catawba in the arms of the Carolinas.
The totality of things will not change, there is nothing else
for it to turn into, one's essence a body made

of elements distributed throughout the entire
aggregate, an admixture of heat. By the harbour
where empties the Mill and the West, Eli Whitney

was credited with the interchangeability
of parts. The beauty and the naming of parts. Revealed
in feeling and abilities, ease of motion

— — —

and the processes. It rides with us into the fields,
among the seeds in the ground. It goes
to pieces on the kitchen table in copper residue,

solvent, and oil. At the summit of his thirtieth birthday party,
he fired four rounds into the rental's drywall
to a purpose mysterious to him. If we are good,

it's because we have recognized goodness. If we are
sharpshooters, it's not because of Christian Sharps
and his patent. Who moved to Connecticut

to become a trout farmer. Ever looming,
Plato's "civil war in the soul." Without extremes
there are no limits. Sighting scope long

as my forearm. Through it may be seen creatures
single and continuous, presenting harmonious
attributes. Once apprehended, they are real

and may be taken. We followed the Henry Repeating
Rifle into the west, and the Winchester
1873. Emptied, the bottle has no reason to live.

- - -

When we speak, the blow inside us
produces a flow similar to breath. Prepare
to kill what you eat and vice versa, he said. If not,

what good are you. It was our better half. By the North
and South Saskatchewan, by the Red Deer and the Bow.
The soul resides in those constituents whose removal

leads to our death. For Christ's sake will you
put that thing down. One day, he said,
you'll crawl out of your hiding place and thank me.

THE ROAD IN IS NOT

THE SAME ROAD OUT

The perspective is unfamiliar.
We hadn't looked back, driving in,
and lingered too long
at the viewpoint. It was a prime-of-life
experience. Many things we know
by their effects: void in the rock
that the river may advance, void
in the river that the fish may advance,
helicopter in the canyon
like a fly in a jar, a mote in the eye,
a wandering cause. It grew dark,
a shift change and a shift
in protocol. To the surface of the road
a trail rose, then a path to the surface
of the trail. The desert
sent its loose rock up to see.
An inaudible catastrophic orchestra

— — —

is tuning, we feel it in the air
impelled before it, as a pressure
on the brain. In the day
separate rays fall so thickly
from their source we cannot perceive
the gaps between them, but night
is absolute, uniform, and self-
derived, the formerly irrelevant
brought to bear, the progress
of its native creatures unimpeded.
We have a plan between us, and then we
each have our own. Land of the four
corners, the silent partner, $500
down, no questions, the rental car
stops at the highway intersection, a filthy
violent storm under the hood. It yields
to traffic from both directions.
It appears it could go either way.

— — —

FORTY

It was a black-and-white episode,
our stroll along the shore road at

Tobermory. Sodium lamps did the best
they could for us in their limited spectrum

and reach, walked us out to the end of the dock,
made a short-armed gesture to the total dark.

You posed on a cache of traps. Seamlessly,
we integrated with the background.

It had been quiz night in the Mishnish Pub,
the river bordering Zambia on the tip of our tongues,

rugby, as ever, an unknown quantity, like the Latin name
for onion. We couldn't pick Lily Cole out of a lineup

if she'd robbed us at knifepoint, and now couldn't see
through to the limits of our sight. A constellation

- - -

of pale boats emerged floating on the air, the horizon
had closed its eyes and disappeared. In this,

our own were not deceived, it's the mind that makes
inferences. When lying in a small room in the dark,

you often survey distances in a kind of daylight,
don't you. You left me sleeping

and went back out to the seawall, the drifting
boats, each a new month awaiting your captaincy.

In the cell water, eye water, the water thought
floats on, rigging clanking softly in the breeze

and afterbreeze, you were anchored
by unseen lines to the harbour.

- - -

LIFE IS A CARNIVAL

Dinner finished, wine in hand, in a vaguely competitive spirit
of disclosure, we trail Google Earth's invisible pervert
through the streets of our hometowns, but find them shabbier,
    or grossly

contemporized, denuded of childhood's native flora,
stuccoed or in some other way hostile
to the historical reenactments we expect of our former

settings. What sadness in the disused curling rinks, their illegal
basement bars imploding, in the seed of a Walmart
sprouting in the demographic, in Street View's perpetual noon.
    With pale

and bloated production values, hits of AM radio rise
to the surface of a network of social relations long obsolete.
    We sense
a loss of rapport. But how sweet the persistence

– – –

of angle parking! Would we burn these places rather than see
   them
change, or just happily burn them, the sites of wreckage
from which we staggered with our formative injuries into the rest

of our lives. They cannot be consigned to the fourfold,
though the age we were belongs to someone else. Like our old
house. Look what they've done to it. Who thought this would
   be fun?

A concert, then, YouTube from those inconceivable days before
YouTube, an era boarded over like a bankrupt country store,
cans still on its shelves, so hastily did we leave it. How beautiful

they are in their poncey clothes, their youthful higher
registers, fullscreen, two of them dead now. Is this eternity?
Encore, applause, encore; it's almost like being there.

ROOF REPAIR AND SQUIRREL REMOVAL

Natural squirrel men, those two,
ladder up the side of the rental, into the attic
before you could say "humane spring-loaded exclusion
device," footsteps confident, efficient,
though they didn't speak, presumably
communicating in the unspoken language
of those born to a trade. We'd never heard a peep
up there. Daily, nightly, the main-floor tenants
pushed their ambient electronica
through the vents, but we hadn't a clue
a halo of chewed wiring threatened us, that the inferno,
as the landlord said, was nigh. Getting used to things
is something even distracted people can do. They thought
they owned the place, but once they leave now,
there's no returning. It's time we were moving on,
ourselves. On the walk, ruins
of what an extended family of nuisance animals
had made its nest from. Shreds of paper,
insulation, twigs from the smoke bush, and the bitter
broken wood of the invasive tree of heaven.

— — —

SAULT STE. MARIE

A storey of blue flame, the "Bay View Candle,"
from the coke stack at Essar Steel Algoma

marks the southwest corner of the Italian
neighbourhood. Flare from blast furnace pipe #7

in the foreground as tractor trailers and students of cheap gasoline
cross the bridge into Michigan as though everything

were normal. Each day a new frontier
to break upon. The fires mean for now there's

work. The drugstore clerk plans to stop in to the casino
for a couple hours after shift and what so-and-so

goddamn doesn't know won't hurt him. She's not talking to me
so I'm inclined to believe her. How difficult could it be

to stay here? Anonymous and thereby absolved.
Everyone's dogs look crossed with wolves.

— — —

A hotel guest is an awful thing, repeating *I'm not from here* into
    the night
while the money lasts. Perhaps it's not contentment

animating patrons of the food court, the sanguine tenor
of my waitress, and the men pray for the burners

to go down, the three days off required to heat them back to
    temperature.
The time it takes iron ore pellets to ship by water

from Cleveland Cliffs, for an epic run at the VLTs,
for mercenaries to shoot 233 protestors in Tripoli

according to the flatscreen above the lobby bar.

— — —

WRAP PARTY

The party planner has transformed the space.
Subtract trousers and voilà, an outfit goes from day to night.
And the bartender's eye elusive as inner peace.

It's your trickle-down economics in action, the crane shot,
the most expensive in the history of film.
We can laugh about it now. This feels like work to me.

The generations' attempts to interface explain
the music. *Last time I saw you, you were wearing a hat!*
Inattention wounds her. Hence, her bandage dress.

There are those you'd rather walk in on in the shower than see
    dance.
But there are good people everywhere, really lovely.
And each of us absolutely wasted, in our own way.

CONVERSION

First impression of a hasty once-over. Of universal
solvent and under-the-bed. An atmosphere both
apologetic and hostile, orphaned
amenities procured at clearance, curtains synthetic

and religious in their weight and ability
to absorb guilt. A thriving ecosystem's residents
stared from fringes of the textiles, the debased
baseboards, and would grow bold. A doorknob

came off in my hand like a joke prosthetic.
Rooms like this have followed me around
for twenty years. It's as though I married into a bad
family of many cousins. I was the only one

who loved them. That's what I thought.
Even as a family steakhouse vented its cruel exhaust
across my threshold, even in the resurrected mystery
of how the moths get in—

— — —

by morning they'd hung themselves everywhere
like little coats by their own hooks—
I was at peace in the luxury of all that lack of care.
It was a skill, like tying knots. When all else

had gone, it would still be there. Blame
for the propane explosion that demolished
the Monte Vista Motel, rendering it only slightly
less habitable, though not registered

in the paperwork, remains, a secret
crouched in the rebuild. In cinder block and flat tarred
roof it rose again, innocent, under the same name, as if
what could accrue had yet to do so. Don't

send me back out there again. That final night
in Salmon Arm, maybe Wainwright, Shaunavon, or
the Sault, wherever it was the last built-in fell out,
or the fold-out fell in, I thought of you then.

Nor is the twentieth century accessible
in Edinburgh. As though, post-concept,
one needs only a velvet rope and a sign
stating it's not here, whatever you came to see.
Move along. Here's Jan Weenix
at the height of his decorative powers, this wall-sized *Landscape
with a Huntsman and Dead Game*
the largest of his allegories representing the senses.
A springer spaniel's inflated proportions
might signify the breed's extravagant stubbornness
as well as a commitment to symbolism.
Misfortune figures in its provenance:
Catholic nuns who acquired the home of an insolvent
sugar merchant sold all five to William Randolph Hearst
whom they entertained and instructed
until his bankruptcy, whereupon it was purchased
by RKO, then Paramount, resurrected as a backdrop
for *Monsieur Beaucaire*, a carefree
adaptation and Bob Hope vehicle

- - -

which delivered unto Hollywood an anxious period of decline.
Taste and *Sight* reside at the Carlyle.
Hearing among the eternal winds
of Ohio. *The Sense of Touch* is lost.
In a clearing, a seaside forest, a typical wooden setting,
the huntsman reclines, back to a tree, alert
to the proximity of his rifle.
Before him, the dead in surfeit are arranged in poses
of sacrifice, liberated even of the void
in their animal souls with which they were content.
They decorate a plinth on which sits a bust of Pan, leering,
externalized, a gaze the tired huntsman evades,
head turned over his right shoulder toward the focus
of the dog's attention, so that all kingdoms
appear to detect the approach
of consequence, and the ugly infinities.

THE MIDLANDS

In an otherwise green field. A black stump
smouldering in a circle of burn. Land

near Doncaster flat enough to make visible a parallel
realm where that thing hasn't happened. The science

of original laws excludes it. Purpose-built
is the mainline from which the long view hastens

counter to the middle distance, and purpose-
built the middle distance, its fences,

hedgerows, ancient oaks lending perspective,
foreground at high speed a series of precise

and irrecoverable losses. Warmbloods, spirits
of immediacy, graze margins of the River Don

heeding its true course through the realities.
They speak plainly. The lie must be inside you.

- - -

LORD OF FOG

It rises from the North Atlantic's stacks
as radio silence, a generalized lack
of discursive tone or narrative movement distinguished
by its density. A mob of spirits enacts freedom of assembly
under a Carmelite aegis. Friendly, to a point; but no
rhythm. The fight goes out of us, highbeams
make it worse. Our dissent voiced frankly in the way
we're put together, in claims to an ill-defined
sixth sense — clairvoyance, gaydar, sensitivity to the dead
and their unending list of grievances —
staring into the infinite regression of our inabilities.
Everything to the right resembles everything
to the left, GPS prompts ring hollow though we were so close
once. Unimaginable speed behaving like stillness.
A confused dream the land entertains. Lay down
your whatever-you've-got-there, don't need to know what it is
to be sure we don't like it. We've no idea
what we've just had a brush with. Unseen
beneath beaded grass tops, the meadow vole pokes

his nose out, scoots among stems of sedges, forbs.
A bad neighbour, his own kind crowd him. Justice
the predaceous gods of land and sky fail to exact in their satiety
or extinction he will carry out himself,

to keep what's his. Full of ire, in rage, deaf as the sea,
he scuttles under cover to the sleeping places of his kin.

DARKLANDS

Reclaimed from brushwood,
from coarse rank grass interspersed
with stagnant bog water,
it's a rich black mould
upon which ruminates
the Georgian country estate,
walled garden abandoned,
antipodal, wanting discipline,
private intentions never more
realized. The door was built
for shorter times. Loose stone
and trippy tufted hillocks spoke
harshly to me. Stinging nettles withheld
ameliorative properties,
broke bottles on my shins.
They supply their own remedy—
who wouldn't like to say
the same? I collected a few
contused apples, impaled

my denim on the blackberry,
stumbled on a buzzard's killsite
as if onto an ashtray in a pile
of paperwork, and that night
in bed imagined a factory
feral and largely silent,
concept and subject both,
fabricating itself out of the initial
qualification from raw principles
of deficiency and excess.
Around it the mad, heavyhearted
wall, the heartbroken
schizophrenic wall argued all
positions. When we're of no more use
we will invent one, a foundation
our own weight dismantles.
I couldn't project my awareness
through the house, it was
too big. Did bootsteps
in the gravel skirting stop at doors
and windows? I was not alarmed,
as the property was highly so,
but would learn I was more alone then
than I thought. At 3 a.m.

- - -

I sat with mobile on the foyer stairs
just inside the door
he stood outside of
speaking into his phone
to a third party, who didn't matter.
We were a single being split
into primary antagonists
likewise inhabited
by opposing pairs, and they
by theirs, so two infinite armies—
at odds but constitutionally identical—
occupied the field
of this decision.
My unknown presence
was my weapon. I waited for him
to initiate the next stage
of our lives.

A GOOD HOTEL IN ROTTERDAM

A baby is crying in a good hotel in Rotterdam.
From the hallway it's impossible to determine
in which guest room the baby cries,
if it does so on the mezzanine,
in the lobby, unfrequented stairwell,
breakfast room, or business centre.
One moment its cries flare behind you, the next
precede you like a herald.
Tonight Oranje will lose to Germany in the Euro Cup
group stage and babies will cry
all over the Netherlands
as parents proclaim their own anguish in the streets
at the feet of the great pre-
and post-war architectures. It's difficult
to sort where the trouble lies, in the public
or private spaces, as you lie in bed
in Rotterdam with the TV on, TripAdvisor
review form loaded on your iPad like a gun to the head
of the good hotel, one of the few

— — —

to survive 1940. To ask why looks for meaning
where there is none. Two blocks away
a Tom Cruise import plays
without subtitles in the Pathé
Schouwburgplein bordered by cranes
pulling the new city from the ground, and bars
that draw like water from the air
partiers kitted out in franchise colours.

TROUBLE LIGHT

Sun of breakdown, sun
in a cage, risen over
a concrete floor, gutting table,
beer bottles. Form
from function dislocated,
the hood is up
in an unsound hour.

Five-gallon pail, rag
and cord on the unshadowed
stage, which is
exclusive. Burning
in the shop in the middle
of the night.
Something isn't right.

— — —

BITUMEN

One might understand Turner, you said, in North Atlantic sky
east-southeast from Newfoundland toward Hibernia.
Cloud darker than cloud cast doubt upon muttering, pacing
    water, even
backlit by a devouring glare that whitened its edges,
bent the bars. Waters apart from society by choice, their living
    room
the aftermath of accident or crime. When the storm comes,
we will see into it, there will be no near and no far. In
    sixty-five-foot seas
for the Ocean Ranger, green turned to black then white as
    molecules
changed places in the Jeanne d'Arc Basin, the way wood
    passes into
flame, and communication errors into catastrophic failure
for the Piper Alpha offshore from Aberdeen.

It burned freely. If I don't come home, is my house in order?
Big fear travels in the Sikorsky. Twelve-hour shifts travel with
    them,

— — —

the deluge system, aqueous foam. Machinery's one note
hammering the heart, identity compressed with intentions,
    drenched,
the tired body performs delicately timed, brutal tasks no training
adequately represents and which consume the perceivable
    world.
In beds on the drilling platform in suspended disbelief,
identified by the unlovely sea's aggression, no sleep aids,
should a directive come. Underwater welders deeply
    unconscious.
Survival suits profane in lockers. By dreams of marine flares
and inflatables, buoyant smoke, percolating fret,
one is weakened. Violence enters the imagination.

Clouds previously unrecorded. Unlocked, the gates of light
and technology of capture in bitumen oozing from fractures
in the earth or afloat like other fatty bodies, condensed
by sun and internal salts, harassing snakes with its fumes.
Light-sensitive bitumen of Judea upon which Joseph-Nicéphore
    Niepce
recorded the view from his bedroom. It looked nice. A new kind
of evidence developed from the camera obscura of experience
and memory, love-object to dote on and ignore. Collectible
photochrome postcards. Storm surge as weather segment,
tornados on YouTube relieve us of our boredom. In the rain,

- - -

drizzle, intermittent showers, unseasonable hurricane
   threatening
our flight plans, against a sea heaving photogenically,
straining at its chains like a monster in the flashbulbs, on wet
   stones
astonishingly slick, we take selfies, post them, and can't undo it.

Meaning takes place in time. By elevated circumstance
of Burtynsky's drone helicopters, revolutionary lenses
pester Alberta's tar sands, sulphur ponds' rhapsodic upturned
   faces,
photographs that happen in our name and in the name
of composition. Foreground entered at distance, the eye surveils
the McMurray Formation's freestanding ruin mid-aspect
to an infinity of abstraction. A physical symptom assails
our vocabulary and things acquire a literal feeling from which
one does not recover. Mineral dissolution, complete.
   Accommodation space,
low. Confinement, relatively broad, extremely complex
   stratigraphy,
reservoirs stacked and composite. An area roughly the size
of England stripped of boreal forest and muskeg, unburdened
by hydraulic rope shovels of its overburden. Humiliated,
blinded, walking in circles. Cycle of soak and dry and residue.

– – –

The will creates effects no will can overturn, and that seem,

with the passage of time, necessary, as the past assumes

a pattern. Thought approaches the future and the future,

like a heavy unconventional oil, advances. Hello infrastructure,

Dodge Ram 1500, no one else wants to get killed on Highway 63,

the all-weather road by the Wandering River where earthmovers
    remain

unmoved by our schedules. White crosses in the ditches,

white crosses in the glove box. The west stands for relocation,
    the east

for lost causes. Would you conspire to serve tourists in a fish
    restaurant

the rest of your life? I thought not. Drinks are on us bushpigs
    now,

though this camp is no place for a tradesman. Devon's Jackfish
    is five-star,

an obvious exception. But McKenzie, Voyageur, Millennium,
    Borealis—

years ago we would have burned them to the ground. Suncor
    Firebag

has WiFi, but will track usage. Guard towers and turnstiles at
    Wapasu—

we're guests, after all, not prisoners, right?

- - -

Efficiently squalid, briskly producing raw sewage, black mould,

botulism, fleas, remorse, madness, lethargy, mud, it's not

a spiritual home, this bleach taste in the waterglass, layered
garments,

fried food, bitter complaint in plywood drop-ceiling bedrooms
strung out

on whatever and general offence and why doesn't anyone smoke

anymore. Dealers and prostitutes cultivate their terms

organically, as demand matures. The Athabasca River's colour
isn't good.

Should we not encourage a healthy dread of the wild places?

Consider the operator crushed by a slab of ice, our electrician
mauled

by a bear at the frontlines of project expansion

into the inhumane forest. Fear not, we are worth more than
many sparrows.

They pay for insignificance with their lives. It's the structure.

Jackpine Mine photographs beautifully on the shoulders of
the day,

in the minutes before sunset it's still legal to hunt. One might,

like Caspar David Friedrich's *Wanderer*, at a certain remove

from principal events, cut a sensitive figure in the presence

of the sublime. Except you can smell it down here. Corrosive

vapours unexpectedly distributed, caustic particulate infiltrates
your mood. As does the tar sands beetle whose bite scars, from
　　whom
grown men run. Attracted by the same sorrowful chemical
　　compound
emitted by damaged trees on which it feeds, its aural signature
approximates the rasp of causatum rubbing its parts together.
The only other living thing in situ, in the open pit where swims
the bitumen, extra brilliant, dense, massive, in the Greek
　　asphaltos,
"to make stable," "to secure." Pharmacist's earth that resists decay,
resolves and attenuates, cleanses wounds. Once used to burn
the houses of our enemies, upgraded now to refinery-ready
　　feedstock,
raw crude flowing through channels of production and
　　distribution.
Combustion is our style. It steers all things from the black grave
of Athabasca Wabiskaw. Cold Lake. Rail lines of

Lac-Mégantic. The optics are bad. We're all downstream now.
Action resembles waiting for a decision made
on our behalf, then despair after the fact. Despair which,
like bitumen itself, applied to render darker tones or an emphatic
tenebrism, imparts a velvety lustrous disposition,

— — —

but eventually discolours to a black treacle that degrades
any pigment it contacts. Details in sections of *Raft of the Medusa*
can no longer be discerned. In 1816, the *Medusa*'s captain,
in a spasm of flamboyant incompetence, ran aground
on the African coast, and fearing the ire of his constituents,
refused to sacrifice the cannons. They turned on each other,
the 147 low souls herded onto a makeshift raft cut loose from
    lifeboats
of the wealthy and well-connected. The signs were there,

risk/reward coefficient alive in the wind, the locomotive,
small tragic towns left for work, where the only thing
    manufactured
is the need for work. Foreshortening and a receding horizon
include the viewer in the scene, should the viewer wish
to be included in the scene. One can't be sure if the brig, *Argus*,
is racing to the rescue or departing. It hesitates in the distance,
in its nimbus of fairer weather, the courage and compassion
of a new age onboard. Géricault's pyramidical composition —
dead and dying in the foreground from which the strong succeed
    upward
toward an emotional peak —
an influence for Turner's *Disaster at Sea*, the vortex structure of
The Slave Ship: all those abandoned, where is thy market now?

- - -

It's difficult to imagine everyone saved, it's unaffordable. Waves
disproportionate, organized in depth, panic modulating
the speaking voice. The situation so harshly primary and not
    beautiful
when you don't go to visit the seaside, but the seaside visits you,
rudely, breaks in through the basement, ascends stairs
to your bedroom, you can't think of it generally then. The
    constitution
of things is accustomed to hiding. Rearrangement will not suit us.
Certain low-lying river deltas. Island states, coastal regions—
floodwaters receding in measures like all we haven't seen the
    last of
reveal in stagnancies and bloat what's altered, as avernal
    exhalations
of mines and flares are altered but don't disappear. Still,
iceberg season is spectacular this year, worth the trip
to photograph in evening ourselves before the abundance when,
    aflame
in light that dissolves what it illuminates, water climbs
its own red walls, vermilion in the furnaces.

PROSPECT

Connected by disposable needle
and tube to a little of this life, a little
of the next, the IVAC complains when its delivery
is interrupted, drags me through an inland sea
up to the human purview: inconsolable
parking lot, aircraft on final approach
above embers of the city that expire
with the dawn as though oxygen's run out.
Workers once banked coals in ashes
leaving for the fields,
the wars, a comfort for those able to return
if they could not. Grief isn't columnar.
It spreads and soaks into the land,
becomes the land. My experience
will prove pointless as any tool used poorly,
the river in its doorway smoking
into cold white air, into the opportunity
of a level place in which to change its state.

— — —

MUSEUM OF THE THING II

And now the objects recur. Chief interests
of their divine secular lives no longer
idle. Thought anticipates them, but they aren't
hindered by it. We have them

in common. They don't aspire.
Appearing in priority, category, scale,
they make possible a world
that does not appear. Arguments favour

their existence. In the rosary of a city block
I find my childhood. I give it away and I keep it.
We were destined for each other, I could learn
from their experience of time

if I could learn. The objects do not defer,
but express themselves as constancy
inside which a seeming shines, surprising
our judgement with affect. We who arrive

- - -

from nowhere in our monotony

of psychic instability, our fragility

and immaterial intuition, contrast sharply

with their variety and richness, plurality

which is the world's first law. Antecedents

and survivors, they are faithful

to our purpose. In them, pretense does not inhere.

If we are deceived, the error is our own.

RURAL CONFLATION SONNET

Pea weevil as eye-headache.
Barbed wire, smart casual.
Four-stroke my electronica.
Clay mud my hospital.

Rattlesnake as concierge,
Lanius, campaign of enemies.
Axe to kerf in contemplation.
East wind my ibuprofen.

Distemper. Disambiguation.
Red oxide as verdigris.
Monsanto our atelier—
From the inside, it dresses me

In esters of phosphoric acid.
The Psalms, a field of grasses.

— — —

FOR THE SKI JUMP AT CANADA

OLYMPIC PARK, CALGARY

You grew into your destiny
in the city's northwest, overlooking
a gas station, the KOA, a few acreages maybe
on the earliest suggestions of foothills,
we hardly remember what that was like.
It was before I was born into
what I think of as my life.

Development has flooded the scene—
Victory Christian Fellowship expelling
exhaust, a warehouse vaguely Bauhaus,
reservoir of modern open homeplans
risen nearly to your base.
Each time I encounter the same place

it's different. The adjacent new
community of Crestmont tries to act natural
leaning on the hill, rife with claims, wearing
last year's colours in its awkward

— — —

final construction phase. In 1988
some people who've bought its houses
weren't yet alive. For them

you might as well be a product
of erosion. A natural event, without promise,
defined according to what is most durable
about you. Does it matter to us
if we're outlived by a minute
or a thousand years? I'm not saying it should.

You strayed from insignia,
from the party of the symbolic imagination,
and no one noticed. Hung with ads now,
the odd corporate zipline. Tourists
on the observation platform observe
the accelerating ritual of supply
and demand. A view makes us feel young.

Ideal conditions are a memory that pains
even a Finn. Competitors and their equipment
have evolved, old ratios are untenable.
You've outlived your design.
Would need to be retrofitted for safety
and who has that kind of time.

- - -

AGAINST LYRIC

Asked for the eight hundredth time that day
if one has remembered to lock the door.
At least, it's not unlike that.

Something contrived from lime Jell-O and Sprite—
coloured marshmallows
suspended like pronouns—

and called salad. Odd, that an excess
should produce such hollowness, tin bucket
racketing down the endless metal staircase within.

Odd my irritability in its fullness should arise
from a poverty of spirit. I could not enjoy
marzipan, either. Half sugar, half

ground sweet almonds, or the cheaper substitute
potato flour, it inhabits as poems do
shapes of pigs, houses, geometric figures,

- - -

fruits whose seeds in nature house
the toxic compound also present
in the bitter almond that flavours it—

your apples, plums, and peaches, stones
and wilting leaves of native cherries—
who count among their symptoms

gasping, the staggers, depression, and death.
Wheeled out on special occasions under
gold-plated anniversary clocks, gilt-

frame mirrors of the commemorative industry,
heirloom burnt-matchstick crucifixes. Faces
around the holiday table chronically etched

in memory's iron ferrocyanide. Churchill
Chelsea Blue Willow dinnerware. Reflection—
there's no solace in it. Because

some of those faces have ceased to change.
Because, now, they will never change.

- - -

SPIRAL

You said a storm makes a mansion of a poor man's house.
I wonder if you did so to make the best of living where
it always blew, the maddening wind that messed up our ions
and made men want to fight. Now you have no house.
There's no need. The cure took the good with the bad.

Who cannot escape his prison but must each day rebuild it?
For a year rather than drink we smoked and went to bingo.
It was like working in a mine, the air quality and incessant
coughing, bag lunches, good luck charms, the intergenerational
drama. It's not my place to say what changed.

You hadn't developed around a midpoint, and fell to the side.
A part remained exposed. Still, you were kind—
unusually so, it seems to me now, for someone with talent.
But loneliness expands to fill the void it creates. To plot against it
was to plot against yourself. You felt the effect of the whole.

When the mind is so altered this resembles death, but it is
not death. Then the faint trail ran out and you continued on.
The night you've entered now has no lost wife in it, no daughter,
no friends, betrayal, or fear; it is impartial, without status.
I would like to think it peace, but suspect it isn't anything.

When our friend wrote you'd died I was on Skye,
where the wind in its many directions is directionless
and impossible to put your back to. He said you'd been living
rough for a while, he wouldn't go to the wake at the bar,
it was too much sadness. That day I'd walked the beach,

picking up shells, their spirals of Archimedes and logarithmic
spirals, principle of proportional similarity that protects
the creature and makes it beautiful. Sandpipers materialized
through tears the wind made, chasing fringes of the rising tide.
At first there were two, then three appeared, but when I began
to pay attention I realized they were everywhere.

MAN IS A RATIONAL ANIMAL

It was the same life, more or less,
yet suddenly a flight itinerary represented
the most tangible indication of my fate.
From the air I saw mountains, forest,
lakes in which dissolved the notion
of ownership, and the sweet little Beechcraft
wagged its tail on landing
in a crosswind. My fellow passengers
claimed their long guns, carried them in cases
like guitars out of the terminal.

Darkness accompanied the second segment,
the Dash 8 traversing the southwest
in high cloud and swinging out over
the Atlantic. Lights might have been
ships, or islands, towns someone
from there could identify. But I wasn't from there.
Where land ended
and the water began was indiscernible,
though I was not afraid. Because I didn't know
what I was seeing.

− − −

THE LIVING OPTION

Having crawled from the desert
of the 1970s already greying a little, impatient,
with physical inconsistencies, crying
bosons and fermions, crying out
the four forces, calling the unified
from the unnamed wastes, it saw in our homes
a vacancy, began repurposing the furniture.
Already it seems never to have been otherwise.
When I think of it my atoms are as the weakening
euro, the housing bubble, too many parts
in search of the one part, it's a joke.
It's a giant scientific instrument outside Geneva.
An argument that knows not me
or my siblings, that has no dominion
over me yet enters my thinking
and undermines it. Then all of my theories
seem raised by the state, fearful,
acting out inappropriately.
                              I went to see you
on an airplane and on an airplane

- - -

was I medicated amid the transatlantic
generation and its complimentary
beverages. People of the light
flying over the living waters. My body,
belted in, a joke, and the heap we call
a mind also, each atom an engine schematic,
a backup system sequence or a prayer
from childhood though I'd lost my faith,
that's how weak I am.
But in the cockpit, threefold,
the Great Invisible Virgin Spirit was incorruptible
in my sedation and in the cabin
the new cashless society
and off the wings degrees
of freedom.

    No patterns emerged
between us, it was new
each time, each event its own, with fresh
odds. We honoured the principle.
Though our creditors didn't see it that way.
They filled our past
with their notices. Their notices
were our bridesmaids. When I think of it
all my atoms are past-due notices

— — —

but with the option to consolidate as one large
debt. The market writes its autobiography
on minds and bodies, my own and those
of my siblings. Are we not innocent
with respect to it? Our credit rating is
a joke, our homes venture with us
through the rental agencies.

                      We went west
before the west dried up. Between Calaway Park
and Dead Man's Flats the cumulonimbus
extended their funnels, melancholy
and inquisitive, they love
the earth so much. Long-haul truckers,
shepherds of product, blew past
on deadline into the storm, tweaking
in their cabs, each cloaked in his machine
with a handgun for an angel
in the lots and roadside pullouts.
If you can't see it, it has
the advantage.

                  If you can't see it,
it's philosophy. A game between us
and the nature of things. People of intent in the valley
of the shadow of. One hundred metres underground,

– – –

a divine heart races in the apparatus
and soon we will hear its voice. It will speak out
from the invisible orders not as an attribute,
a quality or quantity, but a truth perfected
in all the ineffable places. A live
hypothesis. A supersymmetry.
Is it possible to love something like this?
I prayed it might happen to me.

NOTES

"Fables of the Reconstruction" is the title of R.E.M.'s third album.

The title "When Asked Why He'd Been Talking to Himself, Pyrrho Replied He Was Practicing to Be a Nice Fellow" is adapted, along with a line in the poem, from Diogenes Laertius's *Life of Pyrrho*.

The World of "The World" is a cruise liner of 165 luxury apartments owned by a community of residents who live on board as it continuously sails the globe. The poem also draws from Ludwig Wittgenstein's *Tractatus Logico-Philosophicus*.

"Rothko via Muncie, Indiana" includes lines quoted and adapted from a letter written by Mark Rothko and Adolph Gottlieb to *The New York Times* in 1943. The poem was inspired also by *Middletown*, a 1982 documentary series set in Muncie and produced by Peter Davis.

"I Let Love In" is the title of a song by Nick Cave and the Bad Seeds.

The title "All That Is Certain Is Night Lasts Longer Than the Day" is from W. G. Sebald's *The Rings of Saturn*, translated by Michael Hulse.

"Forty" is for David Seymour.

Since "Life Is a Carnival" was written, a third member of The Band, Levon Helm, has followed Richard Manuel and Rick Danko. The title is that of a song by The Band.

"Roof Repair and Squirrel Removal" contains a line from Walter Benjamin's "The Work of Art in the Age of Mechanical Reproduction."

"Lord of Fog" includes a phrase from Shakespeare's *Richard II*.

"Darklands" is the title of the Jesus and Mary Chain's second album.

"Spiral" is in memory of Jim Coates.

"The Living Option" adapts a line from William James's "The Will to Believe" and uses a refrain from "The Second Discourse of the Great Seth," included in *The Nag Hammadi Scriptures*, edited by Marvin Meyer.

ACKNOWLEDGMENTS

I am grateful to the editors of the journals and anthologies in which these poems, in earlier versions, first appeared:

Poetry
   "Bitumen"
The Nation
   "Ode," "The Corners," "Trouble Light"
Riddle Fence
   "Rental Car," "Fables of the Reconstruction," "A Western,"
   "Affirmations," "The National Gallery," "The Living Option"
The Paris Review
   "Museum of the Thing," "Lord of Fog," "Darklands,"
   "Museum of the Thing II"
Eighteen Bridges
   "Rothko via Muncie, Indiana"
The Humber Literary Review
   "Interior," "A Good Hotel in Rotterdam," "Prospect"
Magma
   "When Asked Why He'd Been Talking to Himself, Pyrrho
   Replied He Was Practicing to Be a Nice Fellow," "Your News
   Hour Is Now Two Hours"

- - -

Vallum

"Via"

Room

"I Let Love In," "Lift Up Your Eyes," "All That Is Certain Is Night Lasts Longer Than the Day," "Sault Ste. Marie," "Against Lyric"

Brick

"Keebleville," "Forty"

Studio (online)

"Birth of the Rifle"

The Dark Horse

"Roof Repair and Squirrel Removal"

The Walrus

"Life Is a Carnival"

Cordite Poetry Review

"For the Ski Jump at Canada Olympic Park, Calgary"

Tag: Canadian Poets at Play

"The Midlands"

Poetry London

"The Road In Is Not the Same Road Out," "Conversion," "Spiral"

The New Quarterly

"Spiral"

Hazlitt (online)

"Conversion"

A significant number of these poems previously appeared in *The Living Option: Selected Poems*. Sincere thanks to Neil Astley and Bloodaxe Books.

The Canada Council for the Arts, Ontario Arts Council, Toronto Arts Council, the University of St. Andrews, and Barns-Graham Charitable Trust provided crucial financial and professional support toward the completion of this book.

I'm deeply grateful to Jonathan Galassi for his encouragement and his faith in this book. And to Sarah MacLachlan, Kelly Joseph, and everyone at House of Anansi, for their work and care.

As always, to my family, who are in every word.

Thanks to Ken Babstock, Kevin Connolly, Michael Helm, Michael Redhill, Christopher Richards, Damian Rogers, and David Seymour, for their insight and generosity as readers.

And especially, to James Langer.

— — —